HOW TO WIN THE LOVE GAME

By
C. Alex Anders

RateABull Books

*****

The characters and events in this book are fictitious. Any similarity to real persons, living or dead, is coincidental and not intended by the author. The person or people depicted on the cover are models and are in no way associated with the creation, content, or subject matter of this book.

All rights reserved. No part of this book may be reproduced in any form or by any electronic or mechanical means, including information storage and retrieval systems, without permission in writing from the publisher, except by a reviewer who may quote brief passages in a review. For information contact the publisher at: Alex@AlexAndersBooks.com.

Copyright © 2018

Official Website: www.AlexAndersBooks.com
YouTube Channel: BisexualRealTalk
Visit Alex Anders at: Facebook.com/AlexAndersBooks & Instagram

Published by RateABull Publishing

Table of Contents

Preface 9
1. Introduction 17
2. What Is Love? 18
3. Love Chemicals 20
4. How You Win The Love Game 30
5. Gaining Points 32
6. Losing Points 63
7. How To Stay In Love 70
8. Why You Aren't In Love With Them 72
9. Why They Aren't In Love With You 82
10. Tips and Tricks To Win The Love Game 88
11. Figuring Out What You Want 89
12. Figuring Out What You Like About Your Partner.. 94
13. Figuring out What Romances You & Your Partner 112
14. Revitalizing A Stale Relationship 120
15. Know When To Concede Defeat 127
16. Dealing With Heartbreak 131
17. How To Give Emotional Support 136
18. Wrapping Up 142

HOW TO WIN THE LOVE GAME

Preface

I have something to confess to you. I have never been in a long term relationship. So, you might be wondering why I'm writing a book called 'How to Win the Love Game'. That's a good question.

The truth is that I have thought about this topic a lot. I have a long history of not winning the love game, and it was the frustration that I felt from constantly losing that made me sit down and figure out what it would take to win.

This book looks at love from a neuro-chemical perspective. Often times I will share stories about the things that I've done wrong and why it was wrong. And by reading this book, I'm hoping that you recognize some of your own behavior which prevents you from winning the love game. And I hope that this book puts you on the path to finding love and making better decisions about what you want.

But, before I get to the heart of the matter, I thought I would share with you my challenges with love. They involve a specific set of circumstances which, it could be argued, couldn't have led me anywhere else but here, writing this book. In those challenges, you will see many of the concepts that will be addressed later.

My journey to writing this book had to have begun when I was 13 years old. That was when I hit puberty. That was also around the time that I discovered something about myself that would shape everything about the rest of my life. That was when I began to get signs that I was bisexual.

As a young black, boy growing up in the Bahamas (the country which once banded the movie 'Harry Potter' for being about witchcraft) wasn't easy. It was well known that if the police caught two men kissing, they would beat them up for it. The homophobia was as bad as anywhere in the world, and my starting to have sexual desires for boys wasn't a welcomed feeling.

What made my bisexuality even more confusing was what I would discover later. The truth was that no matter who I met, I never had more than sexual feelings for guys. I had had debilitating crushes on a number of girls along with some sexual feelings for girls. But my feelings for guys remained strictly sexual.

What did this mean? Was I gay because my sexual attraction to guys was stronger than my sexual attraction to women? Was I just a straight guy with wild oats to sow since I felt nothing emotionally towards men? Or, was I just screwed and doomed to either live a lie or to forever be alone?

Another issue which shaped my romantic life was something I'm sure that many of you can relate to. During my formative years, my parents' marriage was falling apart. I witnessed a number of things that a boy my age should never have to experience while forming his self-image. And although I am grateful for everything that my mother has done for me, there is no getting around the fact that her treatment of father shaped the trust issues that I continue to struggle with today.

The final issue that has led me to the creation of this book is something that you probably won't be able to relate to. It took me years to figure out, and once I did, a lot of things in my life made sense. I am what's referred to as dopamine insensitive. Later on, I will deep dive into what dopamine is and how it relates to winning the love game. But for now, I will explain the way our body regulates this neuro-chemical with an analogy.

Imagine a music concert. On stage is the singer and she is singing into a microphone. Behind the scenes is a sound mixer. It is the sound mixer's responsibility to ensure that the audience can always hear the singer, and that the music never gets uncomfortably loud for the audience.

To do that, the sound mixer sits in front of a sound board with a lot of sliding levers. One of those sliding levers is called the gain. When the singer sings a quiet song, the sound mixer pushes up the gain. When the singer yells into the microphone, the sound mixer lower's the gain.

As any good sound mixer will tell you, you don't continuously raise and lower the gain as soon as you notice a difference. A good sound mixer will listen and observe what's going on for a moment. Once they have determined that the singer will be quieter for a continued stretch of time, they increase the gain. And once they have had to lower the gain, they are slow to again increase the gain to baseline levels.

Well, this is how our brain's receptors work. When our body releases neuro-chemicals and hormones, our body's receptors play the role of the sound mixer. When our body is flooded with excess amounts of a neuro-chemical like dopamine, our gain is lowered. And in the case of people like me who are dopamine insensitive, our sound mixers are quick to lower the level of our gain, while also being overly cautious about returning our receptors' levels to baseline.

This condition results in a particular set of behaviors. I'm sure you've heard of adrenaline junkies. They are people who jump out of planes and take unnecessary risks. I'm sure you've also heard of drama queens. They are people who always manage to stir up controversy no matter where they are.

Both adrenaline junkies and drama queens are people who need more and more dopamine to feel normal. And once they lose their high source of dopamine, they will feel depressed, even if people without their condition would consider the same situation thrilling. These people are considered dopamine insensitive.

For years I was dopamine insensitive and didn't know it. The first hints of it were when I was a sophomore in college. It was then when I began working as a professional actor. The pattern which developed was that I would get an audition and it would make me feel ecstatic. I would ride that wave throughout the audition process and the job. But as the weeks would pass without another audition, I would get more and more depressed.

If it took too long before the next call from my agent, things would get dark. I can remember times when I thought about laying on top of the sink and slitting my wrists until the life drained out of me. The thought would grow until my agent inevitably called again. After that, the exhilaration-darkness cycle would reset and the countdown to darkness would begin again.

After graduation from college, the source of my dopamine rushes changed depending on what was available to me. There was a time when I couldn't get enough beach volleyball and racquetball. There was a time when I would ride my motorcycle at 40 mph between the cars on L.A.'s 405 freeway. And there were still other times when I experienced the same cyclical pattern with sex.

It was those three conditions, my bisexuality, my trust issues, and my dopamine insensitivity, which have prevented me from ever being in long term relationships. And, it is those three things that have led me to this book. Freud, the father of psychotherapy, didn't research the mind because he was a well-adjusted person. He did it because he was driven to understand himself.

That, too, has been what has driven me to understand how love works. Without my bisexuality, my trust issues, and my dopamine insensitivity, I would never have been lead down the path to understanding. Now, thanks to what I've learned, I feel in control of my destiny instead of feeling victim to it. Now, I know what has prevented me from falling in love with the interesting, beautiful people that I've known, and what I have to do if I want the life I say that I do.

What you will notice as you read this book, however, is that not everyone needs to fall in love. Love is not the end-all, be-all of life. It is a series of chemical reactions in the body that feel glorious when you're experiencing them, but inevitably evolve over time.

The power of this book is that it puts your destiny in your own hands. You can use the knowledge gained within to understand why you might not have fallen in love with the guy who seemed perfect for you. Or, you can use it to understand why the person you've fallen for hasn't fallen in love with you.

Past that, you will be able to use the information gained within to increase your likelihood of finding love. You'll be able to set up the best conditions for someone to fall in love with you. And you'll be able to move closer to a state of peace about not being in a relationship although the world keeps telling you that you need to be in one.

Choosing to not play is another way of winning the love game. Because, as you will learn, love is simply a series of chemical releases. Those releases aren't limited to romantic or sexual interactions. And knowing that is step one of how to win the love game.

1
Introduction

My biggest pet peeve whenever someone is describing how to play a new game is when they don't start off by stating the game's premise. For that reason, I won't assume that you have the same definition of love that I do. So, in the following chapter, I will do what poets and philosophers have tried to do for a thousand years, I will define what love is… or at least, what it will be from the context of this book.

2
What is Love?

When people hear the word 'love', they think of a number of different things. They might think of the feeling they have for a family member. They could think of the feeling they get when watching their favorite sports team. Or, they could think of the feeling they have for their romantic partner.

All of these feelings are love and they share the same mechanisms that define romantic love. But, for the purpose of this book, we will define love as romantic love. And the feelings which define romantic love will be; ***that overwhelming desire to be with the person we are romantically interested in, while simultaneously feeling the heartache which comes from being apart from them.*** For the purposes of this book, that will be what love is.

As I've stated, all of the other forms of love include one of these two compulsive feelings. The love we have for a parent or child usually involves that heartache we feel when we are away from them. The love we have for a sports team involves the compulsion to be around the thing that brings you pleasure.

What I am describing as romantic love is more intense than either of these two experiences, however. That doesn't make any other form of love less valid or less important. It just makes it different.

And if your current relationship doesn't include those two compulsive feelings, it doesn't mean that there is anything wrong with your relationship. It just makes it outside of this book's definition of love.

Also, keep in mind that nowhere in my definition have I mentioned sex or sexual desire. A desire for sex does not define romantic love. Sure, you might want your relationship to include sex. But this isn't a book about how to win the relationship game or the sex game. This book is strictly about how to win the love game, and you don't have to want to have sex with someone to become overwhelmed by your desire to be with them while feeling heartache when they are not around.

3
Love Chemicals

For some, it might be sacrilegious to limit love to the series of neuro-chemical reactions that cause it. Those who say that might argue that love is more. They might point out the role love plays in the worship of a higher power, and the spiritual connection it can create between two people.

I'm not arguing against that. I think it's possible that love is magical. It's possible that love is a gift given to us by a higher power to experience heaven or the glory of God. But like everyone else in the world, I don't know if it is.

What I do know is that the way our body interacts with love is by the use of specific chemicals. Below I will discuss those chemicals and the role it plays in us falling in love. If you look at the textbook definition of these hormones and neuro-chemicals, you might find something different. That's okay.

'How To Win The Love Game' isn't meant to be a textbook. This is meant to be a user-friendly guide for love. Because of that, I might gloss over the role that some chemicals play in the love game. I'm doing that because if I kept throwing long scientific sounding names at you, at some point your eyes are going to glaze over and the book will stop being helpful.

The purpose of this book is to help you. For that reason, I'm going to limit our discussion to the activities of three neuro-chemicals and three hormones. By keeping track of these six things, you will become your own game master. And you will know how to reshape your world into the world you want.

Endorphins

Although endorphins are one of the most important neuro-chemicals involved in falling in love, I'm not going to spend much time talking about it. The reason is that there is another chemical which we can pay attention to that already has the effects of endorphins calculated into it. It's sort of like how, when playing a video game, your health score takes into account the number of times you've been injured and how much longer you can survive. In that way, dopamine takes into account the effects of endorphins.

But, simply put, endorphins are what is responsible for all of the good feelings in your life. The feeling you have when you're in love is because of a rush of endorphins. The feeling you get after winning a game or doing well on a test is because of a rush of endorphins.

In fact, the reason why crack cocaine is addictive is because it releases endorphins. But, to win the love game, we don't have to worry about our release of endorphins. What we have to worry about is our release of dopamine.

Dopamine

Whereas endorphins are directly responsible for all of those mind altering feelings of pleasure, dopamine is the neuro-chemical that focuses us on the pursuit of pleasure. Dopamine is what clears out all of the possible pathways in front of us and sends us down one path, the one that leads to endorphins.

When you become lost in a good book, it is because of dopamine. When an hour passes by in what felt like five minutes, it is because of dopamine. When we can't stop thinking about someone, it is because our brain has identified that person as a source of endorphins. A large quantity of dopamine is then released to help us obtain more of that wonderful endorphin goodness.

Alcohol releases endorphins. Gambling releases endorphins. Risk taking releases endorphins. And "love" releases endorphins. As a result, our body releases dopamine whenever it seems possible that we can get an endorphin hit.

Now, you might be wondering why I'm choosing to focus on dopamine instead of endorphins since it is actually endorphins which are responsible for that classic feeling of love. That is because dopamine is what creates that need to be with someone which is associated with love.

Why is that? It is because our brain has a way of playing some pretty good tricks on us. We don't actually have to get a hit of endorphins to NEED to be with someone. In fact, not only could your obsession not trigger your endorphins, they could be abusive and cause you harm.

But the chemical that keeps drawing you back to them, and prevents you from getting over them, is dopamine. And for that reason, to win the love game, we will be paying attention to the amount of dopamine our body releases instead of the amount of endorphins.

Oxytocin

Oxytocin has a different effect on us than endorphins and dopamine do. Oxytocin has the nickname, 'the cuddle drug'. It does because a rush of oxytocin is responsible for us wanting to cuddle after sex. It is also responsible for us bonding with others. Oxytocin plays a large role in helping mothers bond with their newborns after birth. And Oxytocin is what is responsible for men bonding with their kids.

Unlike the other neuro-chemicals, oxytocin can be purchased over-the-counter as a nasal spray. Because of that, it is sometimes used by marriage therapists to help estranged couples open up and reconnect. Its effects have also been put to the test by measuring the increased time men play with their kids after a dose.

Although there might be a cascade of neuro-chemicals responsible for a couple's bonding, like dopamine, oxytocin is what we will look at instead of measuring every neuro-chemical interaction.

Cortisol

In every good story, there is a villain. The villain in this love story is cortisol. Cortisol is a hormone associated with all of the bad feelings that we have. When you feel tired, that agitation you feel is largely cortisol. When we feel stressed, it's cortisol. When someone does something to turn you off, that visceral feeling of dislike is cortisol.

Our brain needs a way to signal that we should remove ourselves from situations. Yes, there are neuro-chemicals that could put us on alert and to trigger our heart to race. But being on alert and having a racing heart isn't necessarily a bad thing. In fact, those same feelings also appear when we are in the throes of passion. Most would classify those situations as very good.

But it is cortisol that unequivocally tells us to get out of there. Cortisol makes us feel uncomfortable and worn down. And for that reason, cortisol will be our antagonist in this love story.

Testosterone

I know that testosterone is a hormone that needs no introduction. We have all been taught that testosterone is what is responsible for the development of body hair and the male physique. We might have also been told that it is what is responsible for our sexual desire, but that isn't testosterone's full story.

Although testosterone might be what's responsible for the sex drive in some people. More testosterone doesn't mean a higher sex drive. The sex game is a lot more complex than that. At the same time, though, there is a reason why the myth that more testosterone means a higher sex drive has been perpetuated for so long. It is because of the effect that testosterone has on a person's decision making process and their genital's sensitivity.

It is no secret that genital stimulation brings most of us a lot of pleasure. Using the neuro-chemicals I've already discussed, we can see why genital stimulation releases a lot of endorphins. Because genital stimulation is a known source of endorphins, we release a lot of dopamine when we think genital stimulation is a possibility. And because genital sensitivity can go up with a surge of testosterone, and more sensitive genitals will lead to more endorphins, during a surge of testosterone, we will experience an even greater rush of dopamine.

But, as great as it feels, we can't spend every moment of our lives focused on stimulating our genitals. At some point, we do need to feed ourselves which often means going to work. So, how does the brain prevent us from masturbating all day, everyday? It empowers another part of our brain which is responsible for analyzing the merits of our actions.

When we wake up and wonder whether or not we should stimulate our genitals, the analytical part of our brain kicks in and says that we shouldn't because the dog is staring at us. Once we have taken the pouch for a walk and we no longer have his piercing eyes on us, we might choose not to simulate our genitals because it would make us late for work.

There are times when the analytical part of our brain takes over and wrecks havoc, however. When staring at a gorgeous guy across the room, we might consider if we should go over and talk to him. We might consider where he's standing, who he's talking to, and what his outfit says about whether or not he would be receptive to our advances.

You could stand across the room thinking endless about all of this. Meanwhile, your love interest could give every sign that he's interested before giving up and leaving, all while you continue to weigh the pros and cons. This is an example of your analytical brain being in overdrive trying to figure out your best move.

This is where our friend testosterone enters into the picture. Testosterone doesn't simply make us chase after sex. It slows down the analytical part of our brain to point at which it is practically shut off. A rush of testosterone will cause us to ignore the consequences of our actions. And when the analytical part of our brain is shut down, it allows the pleasure seeking part of our brain to rise to the surface.

Under the effects of testosterone, our brain immediately looks around for the most obtainable source of intense pleasure. If genital stimulation is determined to be the best option, dopamine will flood our brains focusing us like a laser on getting it. If genital stimulation isn't an option, but the rush that comes from a bar fight is, then it will get a friend to hold your beer and some skulls are about to be cracked.

The most important function of testosterone in the love game isn't that it makes you chase after sex. It's that it quiets the analytical mind and allows you to chase after what brings you pleasure. Be that a mate, winning at a sport or starting a new business. Though it isn't the most important part of the love game, testosterone is a very important part.

Estrogen

Another chemical that plays a large part in the love game is estrogen. Like testosterone and cortisol, estrogen exists in a number of different forms. For me to detail each wouldn't help the readability of this book. So instead, I'll mention, in broad terms, the role estrogen plays in love.

Unlike how testosterone shuts down your analytical mind, estrogen can rev it up. Not the entire analytical mechanism, of course, but an essential part. The largest role estrogen plays in the love game is the part it plays in supercharging the part of our brain responsible for reacting to emotions.

It's interesting to hear about the experiences of people who were born female but decide to take testosterone to present as male. A common thing they talk about is that, although they might be experiencing the same situations as they did before taking testosterone, they are no longer as inclined to react to it with tears.

At the same time, when men take estrogen, or experience a condition where their body produces too much of it, they will experience overwhelming waves of emotions. Those increased emotions are almost solely due to the person's increase in estrogen.

Estrogen is important in the love game and we'll go into further depth about it later. But, for right now, that's what we need to know about the three neuro-chemicals and three hormones that control the love game. Now, let's talk about how you play and how you win.

4
How You Win The Love Game

Now that we have an overview of all of the game pieces, it's time to get to the heart of the matter. It's time to talk about how we win the love game. And like every game, winning will be determined by obtaining points.

The object of the love game is to gain 100 points. You can gain those points from two columns; the column for dopamine and the column for oxytocin. It doesn't matter how many you gain from each column as long as it equals 100. And you will lose points if cortisol is introduced to the game.

That seems simple enough, right? That's because it is. The purpose of this love game is to reproduce and propagate the species. It can't be complex. We can make it complex by overthinking it and adding in unnecessary obstacles. But, even within the shifting rules for men and women in our society, the love game has never changed.

5
Gaining Points

So, how exactly do we gain points from dopamine and oxytocin? That's a good question. To explain, we'll discuss each separately.

Dopamine Points

As previously stated, dopamine is linked to pleasure. It's not a direct link, but it is linked. So the things that give us pleasure, or have given us pleasure in the past, give us dopamine points. What are examples of such things?

Just like how birds know to migrate for the winter, and how salmon know to return to their birthplace to lay their eggs, human beings have instincts. Instincts aren't a magical thing. It's just about the way the brain is structured and the physical layout of its neuro-receptors.

That would be one way of saying it. Another would be to say that there are physical objects in our brains which are designed to trigger a particular response.

This physical structure is something which has evolved over time. Our ancestors who didn't have these physical structures were less likely to have kids. The ones that did were more likely to have kids.

As a result, this physical structure has been refined over time. And now, we can point at certain human traits which our society might judge as character flaws, but have played a vital role in our species' survival. What traits are they?

We, as a species, have evolved to experience a rush of endorphins when we see certain forms in nature. There are three in particular. Humans receive a lot of pleasure from seeing things that are balanced. We receive pleasure from seeing things that reflect the curves of a fertile woman. And we receive a lot of pleasure from seeing objects that reflect the shape of a penis.

And it isn't just a male who gains pleasure from the fertile female form, or a woman who gains pleasure from the shape of a penis. It's all of us. The capacity to receive pleasure from balance, curve, and phalluses, are a part of the physical structure of our brain. We can't escape it. And because of how necessary this instinct is for survival, we shouldn't try.

Now, I can only imagine where your mind is going at this point. If you are a heterosexual female, you might be saying that you aren't drawn to the shape of a penis. In fact, you might think they're kind of funny looking. What's more, you might say that you have no interest in women at all. And if you were, by chance, attracted to women, it might be a completely different body type.

That's fair. You might not want anything to do with penises or the fertile female form. But, because we don't want anything to do with it, doesn't mean that our brains aren't responding to it instinctually. We often feel things which are contrary to what we think we are feeling.

There have been studies which have shown that whether or not we like to watch horror movies, or whether or not we think horror movies should exist, the vast majority of us will become sexually aroused when watching them. There has also been a study that shows that women, no matter their sexual orientation, will become aroused watching erotica no matter if it features a man or woman.

These quirks of humanity don't define our sexual orientations or who we are as individuals. They are simply what they are. They are the unchanging parts of the human animal which, socially convenient or not, help us survive as a species.

And, I would imagine that I don't have to go into as much depth about a man's love for the shape of penises. You only need to step into any stall in a public men's bathroom to see that pleasure on display.

Men have built monuments in celebration of the male phallus. Seriously, did no one consider how much the Washington Monument looked like a giant penis when they were designing it? My guess is that they did, and that was one of its selling points.

Again, these instincts aren't bad. They might be socially taboo at this time, but they aren't bad in itself. This instinct informs art and literature. Our drive towards balance transcends its origins in the human face and has become a philosophy for living life. Like every other species, we have instincts. And it is these instincts which are the basis of our dopamine points.

I'm sure that, from what was discussed above, you might be able to guess how a balanced, hence attractive face might contribute to your dopamine points. But, you might not see how one set of traits might trigger a rush of dopamine in one person while not triggering it in others. Here is where things get a little more complicated and where an analogy might help.

Let's say that we were a part of the first wave of humans to cross the ice bridge that connected Russian to Alsaka and hence North America. New to the land, what would be the first things that we would do? Well, we need fresh water and a food source to survive. So, we might decide to send out search parties looking for what we need.

Now, let's say that you were one of those folks searching and you came across a puddle containing fresh water. You, needing the water to keep searching, might use your hollowed out tusk to scoop out the water and put it in your water bag. Deciding to rest for a moment before you move on, you realize that the puddle is slowly filling back up with water. It's clearly not enough water to sustain you or your tribe, but in a pinch, you know you can return to it and get more water.

Because you know that puddle is there, you might allow it to alter your search pattern. Instead of making a beeline into the unknown, you might decide to search the immediate area first. There you might find another puddle and you might find a small flock of geese. You fill up your water bag again and kill one of the geese for food. But knowing this wouldn't be enough to sustain you and your tribe, you move on.

If you are a smart explorer, you would choose to continue this pattern. You might walk a mile from the puddle and geese and circle the area never allowing yourself to be more than a mile away from the resources you've already found. This would be the intelligent thing to do. And it is this strategy that helped our nomad forefathers survive.

Now, let's jump ahead and say that you might not have found one area with all the necessary resources for your tribe, but you have found enough smaller areas, that when added together will feed everyone. What would you do?

The smart thing to do would be to get your tribe to relocate to the center of all of them. That location might be far away from the initial puddle you found, but it doesn't matter. You just need enough resources to sustain you and your people.

This is an analogy of how our dopamine rewards system works. We are born with instincts. The first instinct triggered is the one involving a fertile female. As a newborn, sucking is an instinct and when the right thing is sucked, it gives us food and feeding is pleasurable.

What do we learn from that? We learn that milk engorged breasts give us pleasure. So, as we search the world for new sources of pleasure, we will start off by searching the immediate area surrounding our established source of pleasure.

The breasts that have fed us are our established source of pleasure. We learn that there is a human being attached to those breasts, so that human being becomes another source of pleasure. Soon we discover that human beings can be broken down into the ones with breasts and wider hips and the ones without, so wider hips becomes associated with pleasure.

But as time goes on, we discover that not all females are a source of pleasure. That forces us to find some way of differentiating between them. To that end, you notice that although most of the women in your village are tall, your mother is short.

"There you go. Success," your brain thinks. "Short women bring you pleasure."

So, from that point forward, your brain associates shorter women with pleasure. And, since your brain wants you to have more pleasure, it ties the release of dopamine to shorter women even as the pleasure you get from breasts fade.

The same could be true for the man in your life. As an infant, a man held you and protected you. That protection gave you pleasure. His smell will then become associated with pleasure. His physical attributes become associated with pleasure. Even his way of interacting with others might bring you pleasure.

As you grow, however, and you experience more of the things capable of bringing you pleasure, you don't remain confined to just the things that are most familiar to you. Laughter brings us pleasure, and it brings some of us more pleasure than others. So, we then might be drawn to people who make us laugh.

There is no limit to the things that bring us pleasure and the ways in which we are introduced to them. But, what is most important to take away from this is that these are the sources of your dopamine points.

Let's say that you are a female and, for whatever reason, beards really do it for you. Then a guy's facial hair would be a source of dopamine points. If you really like beards and the man that you're looking at has a great beard, then your brain will automatically give him full points for his beard.

How many points is "full points"? Each individual characteristic can earn you up to 3 points. So, in this case, seeing a man with a healthy, robust beard will give you 3 points towards the 100 you need to win the love game. And seeing a man who is cleanly shaven will give you 0 points in the facial hair category.

Like this, we humans evaluate the physical attributes of everyone we interact with. You might give the girl with green eyes 3 points for eye color. And her size B-cup breasts might reflect your mother's so you give her 3 for that.

The guy you're staring at might make you laugh so you give him 3 for that. But he might have a wonky smile so he only gets 1 point for that.

This is how we gain our dopamine points. For the most part, there is not a lot that any of us can do to change what gives us pleasure. Most of it was determined in our formative years. And the things that weren't determined before age seven, was probably determined by the unconscious interactions we've had with the world.

So, let's say that you are a female and you meet a male. Let's say that his dopamine point profile looks like this:

Balanced face	2
Eye color	1
Smile	2
Body shape	1
Skin smoothness	2
Skin color	1
Muscularity	1
Humor	2
Laughs at your jokes	2
Interesting profession	2
Friendship circle	1
Total	18

By the numbers, there doesn't seem to be too much wrong with this guy. He has a nice smile and a balanced/handsome face. He laughs at your jokes and makes you laugh. There is nothing that is spectacular about him but if your friends were to meet him, they would mostly refer to him as a pretty good guy.

However, if you looked at his dopamine points score, and remembered that you'll need 100 points to fall in love, you'll deduce that you are a long way from falling in love with him. So, what's going on here? Is your future with him destined to fail? Not necessarily. Why? Because we haven't yet looked at this guy's oxytocin points.

Oxytocin Points

The main purpose of oxytocin in the love game is to bond people together. This bonding can be tracked with oxytocin points, and there are three ways you can gain them. You can gain them from; time spent with your love interest, from the emotional support you get from them and give to them. And finally from physical and eye contact, a category which I will, from now on, simply refer to as 'contact'.

Let's discuss each one.

Time Spent Together

What qualifies as time spent with our love interest should be obvious. But in the modern world of Facetime and DMs, things can get a little tricky.

Is texting or messaging considered time together? In short, no.

"Why not," you might ask. "Isn't that a way of bonding?"

Oxytocin can be released in two ways, as an oxytocin rush or as a slow build.

An oxytocin rush typically only occurs in two times in a person's life, after giving birth or after orgasm. And where as the oxytocin rush that comes after giving birth is fairly reliable in women. The oxytocin rush that a man gets after his child is born, is not. Nor is the oxytocin rush that follows orgasm, in men or women.

However, the good news is that for a long time, people have been falling in love prior to having sex. So we don't need to have sex to have an oxytocin release. But, whereas sex isn't necessary for an oxytocin release, sensory input is.

Seeing, hearing, touching, and smelling are all senses that are hard wired to the emotional centers of our brains. When you text, you don't see the person you're communicating with. You don't hear them. And all of the mechanisms which our species has evolved to respond to, are eliminated.

But, I can hear your thoughts. You're thinking, "But, I know people who have fallen in love over text. How could texting not be a love tool?"

I didn't say that texting couldn't stimulate the release of oxytocin. I simply stated that texting doesn't count as time spent together. I will return to the topic of texting later on. Until then, let's discuss other non-conventional ways of spending time together.

Because you can hear them, talking on the phone can count as a way of spending time together. Considering how rare that has become since the popularization of texting, talking on the phone can be considered a non-conventional way of spending time together.

Because you can both see and hear them, Facetime is another way you can spend time together. Doing it, you can become fond of your partner's speech pattern. And seeing them, neuro pathways can develop in your brain that lead directly to your oxytocin centers.

Essentially, any form of spending time together that allows for you to see, hear, touch or smell, your love interest, will lead to a slow buildup of oxytocin points. How many points? That is where things get a little more complex.

Whereas dopamine points were on a scale of 0 to 3. Each of the oxytocin categories is on a scale of 0 to 25. However, you spending every day together for a week won't give you 25 points. You might not even get 25 points after spending everyday together for eight months.

The number of points you'll get will depend on how positive the experience is. If you are in a combative relationship with your potential lover, your oxytocin points will be neutralized by the effects of the hormone cortisol. So, associating stress and fatigue with that person will lower your oxytocin points for them. As will feeling like you are forced to spend time with them against your will.

But more about negative cortisol points later. For now, let's discuss the next oxytocin points category, emotional support.

Emotional Support

By far, the most elusive oxytocin points fall into this category. Giving and receiving emotional support is something that we are hardwired to do. Yet, it is the thing which is socialized out of us the most.

Since emotional support is such a rarity in this time in history, it is probably a good idea for me to talk about what emotional support is for the purpose of winning the love game.

Definition:
Emotional support is engaging in actions which contribute to a person's feeling of worth.

That's it. It's that simple. If you do something that contributes to a person's feeling of worth, you are giving them emotional support. Where the tricky part comes in is in figuring out what contributes to your lover's feeling of worth.

Certainly, there are a few things that are universal. Here are a few examples:

- Listening: When you make someone feel that their emotional journey is important enough to listen to, you make them feel like they have worth.
- Prioritizing: When you make someone feel that their happiness is important to you, you make them feel like they have worth.
- Validating: Words and action which tell them that you value them, will make them feel like they have worth.

A mistake which many people make, however, is assuming that the things that give them emotional support, will give others emotional support.

For example, let's say that when you were a kid, your parent would often drop you to school late. And let's say that it was your school's policy that any late student would have to go the dean's office and explain to the dean why they were late so that they could be let into class.

Let's include that after a certain number of late days, you had to go to detention. And, let's say that the whole process stressed you out.

Now, what would happen if you, desperately wanting to put an end to this cycle of humiliation, went to your parent complaining about them always dropping you off late? What would happen if they ignored your feels on the subject? How much emotional trauma would that cause you?

Certainly, you might realize that there are other more important things going on in the world, and you might choose to suck it up and deal with it. However, you are still human and it will have an effect on you. In fact, your adult partner's ability to be on time when you go out, could become a measure of your self-worth.

What gives us a sense of worth isn't always reasonable, but, it's always logical. There is always a reason for it. If we had a parent who used gifts to give you a feeling of worth, then receiving gifts could become tied to your feeling of worth. If you felt emotionally deprived as a child and you associated that deprival with poverty, then receiving gifts could become tied to your self-worth.

So, there are things that are universal forms of emotional support. But there are also things that are unique to each of us. We don't need to have every emotional need met by someone to fall in love with them. In fact, it's possible to get no emotional support from them and still fall in love. But to get the full 25 points available from receiving emotional support, your partner will need to meet all of your emotional needs.

Receiving Emotional Support

Now that we know what emotional support is, let's talk about your possible points from receiving emotional support. There are 25 possible points available from emotional support. Although there is not a time element required in receiving emotional support, emotional support often takes time.

It can take time for your partner to figure out what form of emotional support you need. And it might take time for you to accept their emotional support. But from the moment you receive emotional support, it can be quite arresting. And depending on how starved you are for emotional support, that sudden rush of oxytocin could go a long way toward helping you fall in love.

Previously I had mentioned that I would return to the role that texting plays in winning the love game. Whereas texting can't be counted as time spent together, your text conversations could be a significant source of emotional support.

The mere act of them texting you on a regular basis could feed your feeling of worth. And if the conversations you have over text gives you feelings of worth in all of the ways you need, those 25 points could be enough to get you to 100 points.

Giving Emotional Support

Although I said that each of the oxytocin points categories is worth a possible 25 points, giving emotional support isn't. That's because giving emotional support is more of a subcategory under emotional support.

You can think of giving emotional support as a category with 10 possible bonus points. The way you get those points is by making the decision to do something for someone else and then learning that it made the person feel better.

This is a category that people often miss. Many times we will give emotional support to someone and the person receiving it doesn't acknowledge its value. There are numerous reasons why they might not acknowledge it, but whatever the reason, the result is always the same.

The person giving the support will either, determine that giving emotional support isn't a good source of oxytocin and will stop. Or, the stress they had to endure while giving the emotional support will detract from their overall love score for the person, and they will begin to fall out of love with them.

Contact

This category is exactly what it seems. Unless they've experienced trauma or a neurological disorder, human beings like skin-on-skin and eye contact. Babies who aren't touched can die. One of the worst things that teens can do to each other is refuse to look at a peer. And as adults, if we are put in solitary confinement and deprived of contact with others, we can go insane.

<u>Eye Contact</u>
Eye contact is so wired into our being that we don't even have to stare into a human's eyes to be washed with oxytocin. Looking into your dog's eyes will not only flood

your brain with feel good chemicals, but it will do the same thing for your pouch.

<u>Skin-on-Skin Contact:</u>
Although touching a person through their clothes is nice and does release oxytocin, it releases nowhere as much as skin-on-skin contact. Touching a person's bare forearm, holding their hand, pressing your naked body against theirs, these sensations are unmatched. And when added to eye contact, the reward for the category as a whole is worth a possible 25 oxytocin points.

Out of all of the other categories, however, contact can also be the trickiest. Whereas receiving emotional support doesn't typically lead to the release of the stress hormone, cortisol, contact can. It is very easy for touch to deduct points from your love score and it happens quite frequently.

Deductions don't only have to happen as a result of your partner touching you too quickly in the relationship. They can happen when we aren't touched in the right place or in the right way.

Lip-on-lip contact should be as simple as it sounds. Yet, if your potential lover is too hard of a kisser or too sloppy, it could introduce enough negative points that you lose interest in them entirely.

Kissing isn't the only form of touching which contributes to your points, however. Light touches on one's forearm, holding hands, oral sex, and intercourse are all forms of skin-on-skin contact which adds to your overall oxytocin points.

Like emotional support, a specific time isn't required to gain contact points. Time, however, is a practical matter. Trust plays a large part with touch. Some of us have more trust issues than others. But for those with no trust issues at all, the 25 points available from contact are readily distributed.

Points from Oxytocin

So, let's put this all together. Here is the oxytocin points profile from the perspective of the female who has met a male. The couple would be the same imaginary couple profiled previously.

Time spent together	5
Receiving emotional support	10
Giving emotional support	3
Contact	12
Total	30

We can see how the early stage of the couple's relationship effects their score. With only five points for time spent together, this could be a couple who have gone out once a week for three weeks and otherwise stays in contact through texting.

The female has given him 10 out of 25 points for emotional support and has only gotten 3 out of 10 for giving emotional support. Perhaps they have gained these point while texting about their day with the occasional complement thrown in for good measure.

They have a 12 out of 25 for contact. That would say to me that they have not gazed longingly into each other eyes, but they probably have kissed and held hands. It isn't possible that this couple has had sex yet. A score which includes sex and orgasm would be at least 17.

So, with a dopamine point score of 18 and an oxytocin point score of 30, and a grand total of 48, you might be thinking that our couple has no shot at falling in love. Not necessarily. Why? Because, in this game, it's possible to earn bonus points.

Bonus Points

Like in many great games, in the love game, it is possible to earn bonus points. Although dopamine points seem very set in stone, it is possible to add dopamine points that aren't related to physical characteristics or personality traits. And although putting in a little work can earn you a lot of easy oxytocin points, it's possible to get even more oxytocin points without putting in any work at all.

Bonus Dopamine Points

Anyone who has fallen in love will tell you that there is nothing better than new love. There is a reason for that. Our dopamine receptors have evolved to search out novelty. The toys you received on your birthday as a kid was never more exciting than the day you got them. Visiting an anticipated vacation destination is never as thrilling as the moment you arrive.

There is a reason for all of this. In the preface, I discussed the function of dopamine receptors using the analogy of the sound mixer at a concert. The down-regulation of receptors isn't something that only happens to dopamine insensitive people like myself. Down-regulation of dopamine receptors happens to everyone. It's an evolutionary feature.

The result is that the first time you meet someone who has a balanced face, and the smile, laugh and sense of humor that you like, you get an extra dose of dopamine simply because it's all new. Within this bonus point system is the glory of young love. So, if you have never before met a boy who gives you so many dopamine points (a first boyfriend), you will get 10 extra points simply because you've never experienced anything like this before.

But the bonus dopamine points for novelty don't stop there. When you start spending time with someone new, you will get 5 extra points simply because they're new to you. When you first start receiving emotional support from someone, you'll get an extra 5 dopamine points from that. And when you first start to touch someone, you'll get an additional 5 dopamine points there.

So, let's take a look at the profile of our imaginary guy who previously totaled 18 dopamine points.

Bonus Dopamine Points – For Novelty

Time spent together	5
Receiving emotional support	5
Contact	5
First Boyfriend	10
Total	25

So, why were these points distributed? Let's say that he is new to the girl's life. That means that he could get 5 more points when they start spending time together, 5 more points when he first starts showing her emotional support and still, 5 more points from when they first start kissing.

That would add 15 points to his meager 18 dopamine points bringing him up to a total of 32 dopamine points. And if he happens to be the first boy that our imaginary girl has fallen for, then he would get an addition 10 points on top of that.

That would bring our heroes dopamine points to a grand total of 42. Add that to his 30 oxytocin points and he's hit 72. And now he's only 28 points short of the 100 necessary to win the love game.

Bonus Oxytocin Points

There are, obviously, numerous ways you can rack up oxytocin points once you figure out what triggers them in your partner, or once your partner figures out how to earn them with you. But there are points you can get without doing anything extra.

As I've mentioned, humans have evolved to crave contact, emotional support, and time spent together. That means that when we don't get those things, we can drop into a deficit. In this way, our oxytocin receptors are similar to the dopamine receptors of a person like me who is dopamine insensitive.

The longer we go without oxytocin, the closer we slip towards depression and the more we crave what we're lacking. If your life is devoid of emotional support, you will intensely desire it. If you are alone all of the time, you will feel desperate to spend time with someone. And if you live in a world where no one ever touches you, you will long to be touched.

That oxytocin deficit has an effect on your total oxytocin points. Because, although holding hands and kissing will always give you 12 points, that would be 12 points above 0. Being deprived of touch means that you are walking around with a negative score. And your negative score in an oxytocin area can drop to as low as -15.

If it has simply been a few months since you were touched, you might have an oxytocin touch score of -3. But if you grew up in a household where no one ever touched each other, you might be in a completely deprived state of -15.

That means that, if you are in a completely deprived state for contact and you are walking around with an oxytocin touch score of -15, and suddenly someone touches you in a pleasant way, you will first return to 0, which is a gain of 15 points. And then you will gain the normal 12 points for someone holding your hand and kissing you.

All of this means that if you are in a deprived state in any of the oxytocin categories, the person who next supplies you with oxytocin in that category, will get all of the points necessary to return you to 0, and then they will get their normal oxytocin points. So, in essence, if you feel lacking in any oxytocin rich areas, the person who replenishes you, will have a greater chance of reaching 100 points in the love game.

Now, let's again take a look at the oxytocin profile of our imaginary woman. Previously she had 30 oxytocin points. But let's say that it's been a year since she has been in anything close to a relationship. Let's also say that her relationship from a year ago was short and not at all emotionally supportive. Let's add that she doesn't have much of an emotional support circle and that she is feeling a little desperate for someone to care about her.

To reflect her state, let's say that she is walking around with:

Contact	-10
Emotional support	-12
Time spent with others	-6

That means that when our imaginary guy does anything to get her out of deficit and back to 0, it will give him a lot of bonus oxytocin points. So, whereas the guy's oxytocin score might have stayed at 30 if she had just gotten out of a healthy relationship, her deficit would give him 28 bonus oxytocin points. Add that to the 72 love points he already had and that would give him 100 points for our imaginary girl.

Even though, on paper, this guy might not be anything special, even though he is barely going out of his way to be emotionally supportive and doesn't have any characteristics that might impress our imaginary girl's friends, our imaginary girl will enter a state where she will obsessively think about him and her heart will hurt when he isn't around.

Although none of her friends will understand it, she will not be able to sleep because of him and she will make decisions that no one in their right mind might make. The reason for that is because, congratulations to her, she has won the love game.

The wonderful thing about presenting the love game in this way is its ability to explain situations that otherwise seem inexplicable. Ever wonder why teenagers fall in love so hard and so fast? It is because the newness of it all is a tremendous source of points.

Ever wonder why an otherwise intelligent friend is in a relationship which is clearly unhealthy? It is probably because the person they're with is taking advantage of your friend's oxytocin deficits. Ever wonder why girls with daddy issues end up as strippers, and guys who didn't get emotional support as kids end up abusively controlling in their relationships?

It is because they are walking around with large oxytocin deficits that are never being fulfilled. So, they act in ways that give them temporary boosts of oxytocin. But because they aren't receiving the boost in the exact category and in the exact way as they have the deficit in, they continue their endless search for relief from their deficits.

Dopamine Deficit Points

Although I didn't discuss this in the section above, I do want to touch on dopamine deficit points before I leave the topic. Just like with oxytocin, we can build up a deficit for dopamine. The process, however, is a little less targeted for the love game in this case.

Yes, if you are fond of laughing and it has been a while since someone has made you laugh, you will enter a deficit for laughing. The same is true with seeing people with balanced faces, or appealing physiques and feminine forms.

The maximum amount of dopamine points you can gain from each attribute is only 3 dopamine points, however. So, if you enter into a deficit for laughing, for example, the furthest you could drop would be to -2. And if the person you're with is causing the deficit, the most that will be deducted from your overall love score is -2.

If you have 42 dopamine points for someone, losing 2 points from a deficit could easily be made up somewhere else. What does become an issue, on the other hand, is when there are a large number of dopamine areas in which you enter a deficit.

If you have been deprived of seeing an appealing female form, with appealing breasts, an appealing waist, and appealingly smooth legs, and then you add that to a deficit for laughter, and the loss of the personality characteristics that drew you to your partner in the first place, then you can enter an overall dopamine deficit. The number of points you will gain when that deficit is replenished will depend on how many deficits are being brought back to baseline.

This dopamine deficit, however, tends to be less connected to the love game and more connected to the life game. If you are walking around in a dopamine deficit, it's possible that finding new love will correct that deficit. But, because the dopamine boost you receive from new love is always temporary, this is a situation where you might be better served to use sources outside of the love game to neutralize your dopamine deficit.

6
Losing Points

So far I have focused on how to gain points in the love game. But like any game, it's also inevitable that you will lose points. Sometimes you can control how many points you lose and sometimes you can't.

How You Lose Dopamine Points

In every relationship, it is inevitable that you will lose dopamine points. That is the nature of our dopamine receptors. Down-regulation is an important part of our evolution.

Above, when I discussed dopamine bonus points, all of those points came from the relationship's newness. It isn't just in the love game in which newness matters. Anything that is new will trigger a release of dopamine.

Have you ever seen a baby suddenly lock their attention on something they haven't seen before? That's the baby's dopamine system in action. Ever see what happens after that baby has stared at the new object for a while? The object loses the baby's interest and they move on to something else. That is also their dopamine system in action.

The thing that might have triggered a rush of dopamine weeks or months before, has a different effect on us as time goes on. Once the novelty of having someone to spend time with wears off, we lose the bonus points associated with it. Once the newness of being touched by your lover becomes familiar, those bonus points are gone as well.

The bonus points aren't the only points you'll lose, however. The excitement we feel from seeing the same balanced face, diminishes over time. The dopamine points your partner gained from having a cool job slowly decreases. And no matter how perfect their fertile female form is, or how magnificent their penis might be, eventually it will bring you less pleasure and their dopamine points will drop.

How You Lose Oxytocin Points

Whereas the loss of dopamine points is inescapable, the same isn't true for oxytocin points. In fact, it's possible that a person might continuously gain oxytocin points over the lifespan of the relationship. But remember, whereas you could earn dopamine points just by being pretty, oxytocin points always required effort. So, to continuously gain oxytocin points over time requires work.

But this section is about how you lose oxytocin points. You lose oxytocin points in two ways. Either, you stop making an effort, or cortisol, the villain in this romance, is introduced.

When You Stop Making an Effort

The reason why the love game exists in its current form is because it works. Yes, it is inevitable that you will lose dopamine points, but you don't necessarily lose all of them. There are certain points which will remain unchanged.

The great thing about making someone laugh is that novelty is built into it. If you tell the same joke over and over again, the joke stops being funny. Any good humorist knows this. So, in order to make someone laugh, you have to change things up. And, if you have the ability to make your partner laugh, you will probably always have that ability. So your related dopamine points don't have to diminish.

But, humor aside, most dopamine points fall, but rarely do they ever fall to 0. That means that, if you've made it to 100 points, you can remain there by making up the difference by increasing your oxytocin points over time. Practically speaking, you'll probably need to max out your contact points, your points from time spent together, and probably both, your giving emotional support and receiving emotional support points to do it. But it is possible.

It is undeniable that maintaining such an effort becomes more difficult over time. It isn't for the reason you might think, however. It isn't because being emotional supportive gets harder over time. It's because it feels harder because we're not still getting the same dopamine rush that we used to get when we first did it.

The dopamine rush we first received was our motivation. As it naturally declines, we recognize the change in excitement and become less interested in giving our partner the contact, time and emotional support they need. That results in a decline in oxytocin and its points.

If either of the partners is deprived of the oxytocin they need, it's possible for them to enter a deficit. And with the loss of most of your dopamine points and most of your oxytocin points, how can love last?

Sure, if you are tied together by debt or kids, you might choose to stay together. But, are you winning the love game? Hell, no.

Negative Cortisol Points

If you remember, cortisol is the villain in this story. If you are a video game player, you can think of it as the big boss you have to battle. Cortisol is the injury you receive during your final fight which, if added up enough, will result in the end of the game.

To get a little more technical, the way that oxytocin works is that every time we meet someone, we create a path in our brain from the image of the person to the part of our brain which releases feel-good and feel-bad chemicals. The feel good chemicals are associated with oxytocin and dopamine. The feel bad chemicals are associated with cortisol.

When you first meet someone you both are getting dopamine and oxytocin rushes, so everything is good. But as the dopamine begins to drop and you aren't so focused on their positive attributes, you begin to notice the negatives. In the beginning, you might even have received lots of testosterone which had shut down the analytical part of your brain. So with the testosterone gone, and the dopamine no longer directing your attention elsewhere, you might begin to notice the subtle ways they cause you stress.

Humans can find patterns very soothing. Often time having a morning routine will allow your brain to wake up at its own pace. Remember, we have evolved to respond to newness with the release of dopamine. Dopamine, will, in turn, cause us to focus on that newness like a laser.

So, let's say that you've been in a relationship with someone for a while. After two years of living together, it suddenly starts to bother you that your partner leaves the cap off the toothpaste bottle. It's a small thing that doesn't matter at all in the grand scheme of things. So why does this bother you?

It is because the misplacement of the toothpaste cap is a break from the path that has been worn into your brain. That change is causing a dopamine release which is preventing your brain from waking up in its desired pattern. The discomfort this causes triggers the release of cortisol. And now, instead of associating nothing but positive neurochemicals with your partner, you are beginning to associate negative ones.

These negative associations are your negative cortisol points. One negative cortisol point will cause the loss of one oxytocin point. Get enough negative cortisol points, and you could end up in an oxytocin deficit which might not only cause you to fall out of love, but might make you hate them.

The cap on the toothpaste is always a fun example of why a relationship could fall apart, but most are more serious. Money stress can rob you of oxytocin points. Work stress and child rearing stress can do the same.

Anything that causes the release of cortisol, be it mental health issues, safety issues or simple logistical issues, will eat away at your oxytocin points and ensure that you lose the love game.

7
How To Stay In Love

You might be wondering now, how it is that you could win the love game over the long run given all of the obstacles. The natural drop in dopamine alone can be a one man game changer. Were we even supposed to win the love game, or was the game designed for us to lose?

Believe or not, in spite of my relationship history and all of the things preventing us from winning, I think that the love game was designed for us to win. There are many people in the world who are in relationships that last decades and are still winning the love game. What is true with them, however, is that the source of their 100 points changes over time.

Dopamine is a very useful neuro-chemical for shaping people's behavior. The fact that dopamine is released when we first spend time with people is no coincidence. Neither is the release of dopamine when we first give and receive emotional support, or when we touch someone for the first time.

These dopamine spikes are the encouragement we need to explore the activities that will release oxytocin. If nurtured, oxytocin will be released at high levels until we die.

If you are maximizing your oxytocin points, then you don't need many dopamine points to remain at 100. So, as long as your partner retains enough of their looks or humor to make up the remaining points, you might be able to sail through life as one of the true winners of the love game.

8
Why You Aren't In Love With Them

I imagine that, at this point, your head is spinning a bit. 5 point because of this. 10 points because of that. It's a lot to keep in your head. But it's easy, I swear.

What we need to do to lock all of this information in, is see the love game in action. Using it to answer your most burning questions is the best way to practice using it while explaining your entire romantic life.

In this section, I'll give common relationship scenarios and use the love game to explain why you might not be in love with the great guy you've met. Perhaps your friends call you too picky. Perhaps you don't understand why you aren't falling for the person who checks all of your boxes. No, you aren't broken. It can all be explained, so let's begin.

Why I haven't Won the Love Game

I started out the book by discussing my relationship dilemmas. I mentioned that I had never been in a long term relationship. But what I didn't mention was the enormous amount of frustration it has caused me over the years.

My lack of relationships has taken me to some dark places. It has caused me to think that I was broken. It made me believe that I had no chance at love. But it turns out that my situation was the natural outcome of the things I've already described. Let me walk you through my situation in the hopes that it will give you insight into your own.

As a 6'5" guy whose mother was a Miss Universe contestant, I deserve no credit for winning the genetic lottery. But what that meant was that I've never had that hard of a time attracting the attention of both men and women (remember, I'm bisexual). But don't jump to any conclusions about the ease of my life, because everything has only worked against me when playing the love game.

At the heart of my problem was my parent's sometimes rocky relationship. What I learned from watching them was that I couldn't trust others, because if I did, I would be hurt. What did that do? It associated a release of cortisol with intimate situations.

Because cortisol makes us feel bad, we tend to avoid it. Because we have evolved to need intimacy, we can't avoid it completely. But if intimate situations bring on stress, the best compromise is that you avoid it as much as we can.

This is a common experience that people have, so I'm sure this pattern seems familiar. But, in spite of others experiencing the same thing, they don't go through life avoiding relationships. The usual course is to reluctantly get into a relationship and battle your trust issues while satisfying your need for contact, and time spent together.

This is true. But where I differed was that I was dopamine insensitive. In most people, the rush of dopamine that comes from being with someone attractive and having sex with them for the first time will make you want to spend more time with them. It takes a few weeks for the dopamine to start to down-regulate for most people. But because I am dopamine insensitive, my drive to spend time with them would drop too quickly.

The result would be that I would lose my drive to be with them before our time spent together and contact would build up enough oxytocin to encourage the acceptance of emotional support.

The other issue I experienced which made a long term relationship almost impossible for me stemmed from my bisexuality. Bisexual attractions take different forms. Very few bisexuals are equally attracted to men and women.

My situation is that I have a slightly higher physical attraction towards the same sex and an almost exclusive desire for long term relationships with members of the opposite gender. That almost exclusive desire, plus my trust issues meant that I couldn't get to 100 with either gender.

Men, who gained a lot of dopamine points, would gain 0 emotional support points, almost 0 time spent together points and just the points attributed for sex. And because I am dopamine insensitive, and my dopamine receptors get down-regulated very quickly, I would lose interest in those guys and move onto someone new.

Women, on the other hand, wouldn't trigger as many dopamine points during our first meeting. It would take me a while to discover the qualities that delivered dopamine points, and that wasn't necessarily a bad thing. But because I didn't have ready access to all of those initial dopamine points for physical characteristics, I became more dependent on oxytocin points to make things work.

That is where my trust issues would come into play. When you have trust issues, you don't necessarily want to spend a lot of time with your potential love interest. Increased time together would give them too many opportunities to hurt you. Opening up is the bases of receiving emotional support and opening up gives your partner ample ways of hurting you. And where as sex is fine, when you are closed off emotionally, you aren't that interested in holding someone's hand as you walk down the street.

The result of all of this was that I didn't have enough oxytocin points with guys and I didn't have enough dopamine or oxytocin points with women. Perhaps this isn't exactly what you are experiencing, but, odds are that you'll find something familiar in your own story.

For years, I have beat myself up about my lifetime of short-term relationships. Now I understand that, considering all of the circumstances, my history of short-term relationships was inevitable. It wasn't that it was impossible for me to win the love game. It was that I needed to know the way the game worked in order to have a shot at winning.

For most people, love happens the same way. You meet someone you find attractive. You spend time with them and begin giving and receiving emotional support. You fall in love with them until your dopamine points drop. And then you determine if you have enough oxytocin points to build a lifetime together. If you decide that you do have enough points, you enter into a long term relationship. If you don't, you break up.

If you have issues that prevent you from spending time together, giving and receiving emotional support, and touching each other, you will be completely reliant on dopamine points to maintain your relationships. But because dopamine receptors have evolved to down-regulate over time, you will have no shot at winning the love game.

Other Things that Prevent You from Falling in Love

Although mine might be an extreme case, I'm sure that there are aspects of my story which are familiar. How many times have you met someone where there wasn't an immediate "spark"? Was it on a date? Was that lack of "chemistry" what led to no second date? Well, let's now explore what "having a spark with them" means.

When There is No Spark

Take a moment to consider the people you've had and haven't had sparks with. What were the differences? If you made a list of each of their dopamine points, what would be each of their scores?

Did a physical characteristic result in 3 points? Did each of the candidates have it? Is there a particular body shape or style of humor which always results in 0 or negative cortisol points?

Ultimately, "having a spark" is a folksy way of describing the increased focus we give someone because of high dopamine points. When we talk about sparks, we usually aren't even taking into account the other person's experiences. We are talking about our own while hoping the other person is experiencing the same. But because we're hopped up on dopamine points, we have a hard time seeing that.

So, what's the one reason you aren't falling in love with a potentially great guy? Is it because of the lack of a magical "spark"? No, it's because they aren't giving you enough dopamine points.

But let's say that you felt enough of a spark to continue to go out with them. Let's say that you've gone out with them a couple of times and you might have even kissed them. You might be thinking that the kiss is what would have told you one way or the other. Isn't that the way it works? If you don't feel it with the kiss, you never will, right?

Well, there is a reason why so many women feel like they know after a kiss. It is because men can transfer testosterone in their saliva as they kiss. The recipient of that testosterone filled saliva will associate the testosterone rush they feel with the kisser. That testosterone will, in turn, quiet the recipient's analytical mind and make their genitals more sensitive. This will, in turn, boost the recipient's dopamine and increase their dopamine points.

On the other hand, if the recipient is used to kissing people who transfer testosterone and none is transmitted, they might blame it on a lack of chemistry between them. Is that true? Can you assume that the only reason a person wouldn't transfer testosterone in their kiss was that they aren't really into the person they're kissing? No, you can't.

There are a number of reason why the other person might not have an excess of testosterone in their saliva as they kiss you. They could be feeling stressed about initiating the first kiss. Increased cortisol decreases testosterone. They could have lower levels of testosterone to begin with.

However, if you are looking for signals like this to tell you whether or not you could love them, then you might miss all of the oxytocin points and bonus dopamine points you get from time spent together and emotional support.

When All They Have are Their Looks

Another reason you might not be falling in love with your partner is that, in spite of the high number of dopamine points they give you, their lack of emotional support and time spent together is preventing you from reaching 100 points.

Is it possible to reach 100 with only dopamine points? Yes. But, not only is it rare, it has 0 chance of lasting. Oxytocin is what makes you long for someone when they aren't there. That is half of the equation for winning the love game.

There are a number of examples I can give as to why you aren't falling in love with the person you're with. But ultimately, it comes down to a lack of dopamine or oxytocin points. And whereas dopamine points are what they are, often times the reason you might not have enough oxytocin points is that you're not spending enough time together, you aren't giving and receiving enough emotional support, or because you're not making enough skin-on-skin, or eye contact.

It is also possible that too many negative cortisol points are being introduced into the relationship. For that reason, you often need more than 100 points to stay in love. And if your partner causes you stress, or your life stress is spilling over into your relationship, it might be impossible to continuously win the love game.

9
Why They Aren't In Love With You

The reasons why someone might not fall in love with you are obviously the same reasons why you might not fall in love with someone else. But, in this section, I will go over some of the reasons you might not readily think about while you are under the effects of a lot of dopamine points.

Lack of Dopamine Points

As I state previously, there are characteristics which are universally attractive. We are all helplessly drawn to a balanced face. It could be an adult's, a baby's, or even a dog's. We are even drawn to paintings with symmetry. We can't help it. It's who we are as a species.

But, because we are all drawn to it doesn't mean that we have positive associations with it. If classically attractive people picked on you in high school, you may not allot them 3 dopamine points as an adult. And if something so ingrained into our species can't always give you 3 points, then what can?

The answer is nothing. There are no characteristics that everyone in the world will say is worth full dopamine points. There is no body type and no style of humor. No matter who you are, there are going to be people who don't allot you many dopamine points. Whether it be because of eye color, height, weight, skin complexion, or your profession, you are not going to score 3s across the board.

Consider how, even with your biggest crush, there was something about them which was only okay. Sure, you might not have been able to focus on it while you were lost in the storm of dopamine, but now it should be clear. So, if a person who seemed to be perfect for you, could come up short, then obviously, you not triggering enough dopamine points in every situation has to be acceptable.

And, you can rest assured that if your crush gives 1 dopamine point for someone under 5'10", you can't convince them to give you 2 points instead. If a person never gives someone more than 1 point for hair style, no matter how much you change your hair, you are not going to get more than 1 point for it.

This inability to increase your dopamine points in the mind of your partner might seem disheartening. But try not to think of it that way. Think of it instead as being something that is in no way your fault. So many people think that if they were thinner or richer, all of their relationship issues would be solved. That is so often not the case.

If you get 0 points for body shape, what does it matter? It's only one category. There's still the category of eye color, smile, sense of humor, and even hand size that could gain you points. The only way one category could be a deal breaker is if they associate one of your characteristics with a lot of negative cortisol points. And if you can offer them enough oxytocin points, those cortisol points can be overcome.

Lack of Oxytocin Points

The other major reason why they might not be falling in love with you is that they don't get enough oxytocin point from you. That could be your fault, or it could just be a matter of circumstances.

Perhaps you live too far away for you to give them oxytocin points for time spent together. Perhaps they're a secret introvert and all of the time you're spending together is stressing them out and adding negative cortisol points.

Perhaps they aren't willing to give you emotional support. Perhaps they are trying to give you emotional support, but you aren't acknowledging it in a way that registers with them.

As I've stated, along with the typical ways, we all have specific types of emotional support that we prefer. Your potential partner could be offering you emotional support by always texting you right back. But because you don't value a prompt response, you might not close the loop by acknowledging their actions. Without that acknowledgement, they won't add oxytocin points to your score.

Or perhaps you've figured out what type of emotional support they need. But every time you try to offer it to them, they reject it. That happens. No matter your effort, there are just some people who aren't capable of receiving emotional support.

I know this because I was one of those people. You could compliment me, you could be there for me as much as you wanted. But my life had taught me that trusting people resulted in stress. Therefore, I didn't trust people and I rejected everyone's offer of emotional support.

A final reason you could not be getting enough oxytocin points involves skin-on-skin contact. As I've stated, not all touching is equal. Whether we're male or female, we've all gone through experiences which have shaped our feelings surrounding being touched. Yes, some of us simply get stressed when we are touched. But it's not always so black and white.

Certain types of touching will give us more oxytocin points than others. For some of us, hand holding is what would max out our oxytocin points. For others of us, it's massage. But even for those who think that sex is the end-all-be-all source of oxytocin points, you have to ask, 'what type of sex will release it?'

Will you only trigger oxytocin points through oral sex? Would it be intercourse? And for those who need a mixture of both, does the ratio of oral sex to intercourse matter and are they only achieved in unusual circumstances like when they are wearing their socks?

Just like we have specific forms of emotional support which result in the greatest effect on us, we all have ways of being touched that give us the most oxytocin points. And, you might think that this is something you could simply ask, but that's not always the case.

One of the key reasons you usually aren't able to give your partner what they need for their oxytocin points is because they don't know themselves. Often times we fall back onto what people tell us we should like or want. We are individuals, however. And even when you are doing what they have told you that they want, you might not be getting any closer to winning the love game.

Hey, I never said that winning the love game is easy. Understanding the game is easy. But humans, as a species, are complex. Each of our particulars is as varied as snowflakes. But, luckily, there is more than one strategy for winning the love game. We just need to play with a partner with which it's possible to win.

10
Tips & Tricks
To Win The Love Game

I hope that you have found my description of the love game helpful. I know that it has been tremendously helpful in my pursuit of happiness. The biggest surprise to me in its discover was how much angst it releases by simply knowing how the game works. What it taught me was that I'm not helpless to my circumstance. In fact, I have a tremendous amount of control over how my love game is played.

What I have also discovered since learning the rules, are the ways to use the rules to my advantage. What follows are my tips and tricks on how you can more easily win the love game.

11
Figuring Out What You Want

One of the hardest things in life is figuring out what you want. I will acknowledge that now before I casually insist that you should figure out one of life's greatest challenges. But, never-the-less, the difficulty of it doesn't take away from the necessity of it. And even if, at this moment, you can't pin point exactly what you want, at least get the process started so that you're not starting from scratch ten years from now.

The great thing is that once you understand the love game, you have a framework to understand the rest of life. I explained the dopamine point system in the context of finding love, but that is how dopamine works for all aspects of our life.

We assign points to the things that give us pleasure, whether it's assignments at our job or our decision to volunteer our time. And using the understanding I've presented above, you can begin to rate things by the amount of pleasure something gives you in relation to the amount of stress it generates.

Although it would be nice to figure out what you want out of life, what I was really referring to when I suggested that you figure out what you want, was really in relation to love. Be honest with yourself, are you a person who gets a tremendous amount of pleasure from being chased or from chasing others? Does it give you a rush that is beyond anything you feel once you are caught or you've caught your prey?

If you do get pleasure from being chased or chasing others, be comfortable with that. Own it. There is nothing wrong with that. Sadly, we don't have that much to do with the way our brains have developed. You are the way you are. The only moral crime comes when you knowingly hurt others for your selfish gain. Avoid that and you're golden.

Adding to that, if you are a person who wants emotional support and intimacy, it's important to really understand that. Why? Because you might be doing things to spike your dopamine points not realizing that it is sometimes sabotaging your chances of getting the emotional support you desire.

Here's an example. For this, I have to revisit the roles that testosterone and estrogen play in the love game. Women usually have much more estrogen than men. Estrogen ramps up your emotional processing making emotional support particularly pleasurable.

Testosterone, on the other hand, shuts down our analytical and emotional mind. Men usually have more of it than women, and testosterone can be triggered when we see things associated with our three core instincts, balanced faces, fertile female forms, and penis shapes. The structure of our brain will determine how much testosterone is released in each case, but it tends to be greater than 0 for everyone.

So, if you are a woman craving emotional support and you are interested in getting it from a man, you might decide to use your fertile female form to get him. What would be the result of that?

If the man you're interested in gives a lot of dopamine points for fertile female forms and the qualities that go along with it, you might spike their dopamine enough to get them to pay attention to you. But, what is released in addition to the dopamine? Testosterone. And that testosterone will shut down the man's analytical and emotional centers making them unable to offer you the emotional support you crave.

Having a sexy partner is great. We all love sexy. But if every time your partner sees you, they think of sex, it will be impossible for you to get what you're after.

The first step to getting what you want is figuring out what you want. Do you want short term relationships based on lots of dopamine points? Do you want a relationship which is primarily emotionally supportive? Do you want a mixture of both? If you do, what ratio of dopamine to oxytocin points would you prefer? What ratio of dopamine to oxytocin points would you be willing to live with?

And remember, if you say that you want 50 of your 100 points to come from oxytocin points, that would be out of the available 85 oxytocin points. There would be 35 points that they aren't giving you. That means that, either they're not always emotionally supportive, they don't always touch you the way you like, or they don't spend as much time with you as you would want.

And, if you say that you want 85 of your 100 points to come from oxytocin points, that means that they are only giving you 15 dopamine points. So, they might not be as sexy as you want them to be, or as tall, or as funny. And, you know what, not only might their friendship circle be annoying to hang out with, but their income potential might suck.

So, again, what ratio of dopamine to oxytocin points would you prefer, and what ratio would you be willing to live with? Once you have figured that out, write it down and give some thought to what you might have to do to get it.

12
Figuring Out What You Like About Your Partner

Once you have figured out what you want, compare what you want to what you have with your partner. Do you have 100 points with your partner? In what ratio of dopamine to oxytocin points? Does your partner have a lot of dopamine points based on the newness of your relationship? What will happen once those newness points drop off? Will you still have 100?

For this, it might be helpful to take some time and chart out your partner's dopamine and oxytocin points.

Calculating Dopamine Points

Below, I have included a partial list of areas in which you might give your partner dopamine points. The way to determine points would be based on how much that characteristic matters to you and how close your partner is to your ideal.

So, for example, let's say that you know that a sense of humor could bring you boundless pleasure. And you know that your partner makes you laugh endlessly. Then you need to give your partner 3 out of the possible 3 points for sense of humor.

On the other hand, let's say that you really don't feel that the shape of your partner's thighs is important to you. In this case, no matter the shape of your partner's thighs, you have to give them 0 points for that category.

Remember, dopamine points are allotted based on how much that characteristic excites you. If thigh shape doesn't excite you, then your partner's thigh shape can't give you any dopamine points.

Physical Appearance	0-3 pts
Height	
Overall body shape	
Face balance	
Hair color	
Hair fullness	
Hairline	
Body hair	
Skin tightness	
Skin smoothness	
Eyebrow shape	

Eye color	
Eye shape	
Cheekbone prominence	
Lip fullness	
Smile	
Teeth	
Chin prominence	
Chest shape	
Shoulder size	
Back shape	
Biceps	
Forearms	
Wrists	
Hands	
Waist shape	
Hip size	
Buttock size	
Genital shape	
Thigh shape	
Calf shape	
Ankles	
Feet shape	
Feet size	

Personality

Sense of humor	
Enthusiasm about life	
Adventurousness	
Spontaneity	
Cheerfulness	
Intellect	
Generosity	
Seriousness	
Stability	
Relatability	

Talent	

Externals

Friendship circle	
Job	
Income potential	
Financial stability	
Home ownership	
Settling down potential	

Calculating Oxytocin Points

Also, take a look at your partner's oxytocin points. Remember, oxytocin points are allotted based on how much and how often they have made you feel fulfilled in that area.

Calculating 'Time Spent Together' Points

For 'Time Spent Together', let's say that the minimum time period necessary to get full points is two years. And for every five years after that, you can add two bonus points. This will make it possible to exceed 25 points if you've been with your partner for decades.

So, ask yourself, what percentage of your non-work, non-sleep time is spent with your partner. If all of your non-work, non-sleep time during the past two years was spent with your partner, then they deserve the full 25 points. If it was less, then adjust your score accordingly. And don't add in the negative points for too much time spent together. We will add that later.

	0-25 pts
Time spent together	

Calculating 'Receiving Emotional Support' Points

To determine their score for emotional support, ask yourself how emotionally supported you feel and how much of that comes from your partner. If you feel completely emotionally supported, but none of that is coming from your partner, then your partner gets 0. If you feel you get half of the emotional support that you need and your partner is only responsible for a half of that, then you should only give your partner 25% of the possible 25 points.

	0-25 pts
Receiving Emotional Support	

Calculating 'Giving Emotional Support' Points

If you feel that you give all of the emotional support that you can think of and your partner makes you feel like the best person in the world for it, then give them the full 10 points for how they respond when you give them emotional support. If you give them emotional support whenever you think about it and they make you feel like a champ for it, then give them 10 out of 10 points for it.

But, if you give them emotional support and they only acknowledge your effort half the time, give them half the points. And if you never make an effort to give them emotional support or if they never acknowledge the support you give them, give them 0 points. You can always allot them points which are somewhere in between.

	0-10 pts
Giving Emotional Support	

Calculating Contact Points

There are two types of contacts which can gain you points, eye contact, and skin-on-skin contact. Your points from eye contact are determined by two factors, duration, and frequency. Your points for skin-on-skin contact are determined by three factors, duration, frequency, and by who's touching whom.

Calculating Eye Contact Points

We all have different durations of eye contact that we're comfortable with. But, generally speaking, the more eye contact you make, the more oxytocin points you gain. To make it easy, let's say that maintaining eye contact for five seconds or more will give you one point.

Rarely do we maintain eye contact for more than five seconds, but when we do, the rewards increase. If your eye contact exceeds 15 seconds, you will gain another point. Every 15 seconds after that, you will gain another point. And if you are capable of maintaining eye contact for three minutes, you will max out your eye contact points at 12.

Along with the duration of the eye contact, the frequency is also important. Eye contact has a window to gain points after which the points will drop off. In spite of what Shakespeare says, we weren't meant to forever fall in love with someone simply by gazing at them. So, we will gain and maintain eye contact points for two weeks intervals. After that, the points will go away and we will need to reacquire them.

Luckily, staring into our partner's eyes is a well that will never go empty. The reason why we tend to stop doing it as our relationship continues, is because of our drop in dopamine. Once our decline in dopamine points causes us to turn our focus elsewhere, we stop doing the things that don't feed our hunger for endorphins.

Oxytocin is a warm, relaxed feeling that consumes us like a bath. But nothing compares to the unadulterated pleasure that comes from an endorphin rush.

Calculating Skin-on-Skin Contact Points

The first thing to consider when calculating oxytocin points from skin-on-skin contact is who is touching whom. You touching them is only worth half of the points of them touching you. Also, duration and frequency of touch are important. If they touch you for more than five seconds, they get a point. For every hour block that they touch you for more than five seconds, they will get another point.

Kissing, on the other hand, will give them 3 points. Oral sex will give them another 3 points. Intercourse, which usually includes sustained skin-on-skin contact, will give them 3 more oxytocin points. And if you orgasm because of sex, you will gain an additional 5 points.

Like with eye contact, these points won't last forever. The points from really great sex will remain on your leger for two weeks. After that, those points will slowly drop off. After a month, they aren't completely gone, but it's close to it.

Combining eye and skin-on-skin contact points, you can only ever gain 25 oxytocin points. However, it is possible to gain bonus contact points. And those bonus points can be permanent causing you to think about your partner for the rest of your life.

Contact Points	0-12 pts
Eye contact	

Contact Points	0-25 pts
Skin-on-skin contact	

Calculating Bonus Points

There are two way you can gain bonus points. You can gain dopamine points from the newness of your relationship. And you can gain oxytocin points from the maturity of your relationship.

Calculating Bonus Dopamine Points

Bonus dopamine points are distributed for the newness of a relationship. So, for each of the three oxytocin categories that have at least 1 point, add a bonus 5 points.

So, for example, if you are receiving any emotional support at all, then add 5 bonus points for the emotional support category. If you two have spent anytime together at all, you get another 5 points. And if you two have made eye or skin-on-skin contact for more than five seconds, you get another 5 bonus points.

However, since these are newness points, your bonus points disappear the longer you're with them. In fact, you only get 5 points if your relationship is less than a month old. For every month after that, you subtract a point.

So, if your relationship is between 31 and 60 days old, you only get 4 points. Between 61 and 90, you only get 3 points, etc. And, by the time you hit six months, the newness of it all is gone and you will no longer get newness bonus points.

Bonus dopamine pts	0-5 pts
Time spent together	
Receiving Emotional support	
Touching	

Calculating Bonus Oxytocin Points

Bonus oxytocin points are gained because, after a while, regularly used oxytocin pathways are permanently burned into our brains. That is why, years after a breakup, you will continue to think about an ex. And those permanent oxytocin points must be accounted for in your score.

So, for every five years that you have at least 1 oxytocin point in a category, add 2 permanent oxytocin points. That means, if you have at least 1 Time Spent Together point every day for five years, add 2 bonus points. However, if at any time during a five year span, an oxytocin category had a negative score, they won't get the bonus 2 points.

Bonus oxytocin pts

Time spent together	
Receiving Emotional support	
Touching	

You might be wondering how an oxytocin category might end up with a negative score. That's easy. It's because of negative cortisol points. A negative represents a state of deprivation. Let's now discuss what causes deprivation and calculate the negative cortisol points you have for your partner.

Calculating Negative Cortisol Points

Cortisol can affect our dopamine points as easily as our oxytocin points. It is the stress hormone, and cortisol is usually unpleasant to experience. As unpleasant as it is, however, it isn't as powerful as you might think. No single injection of cortisol can eliminate 100 points. What it can do, though, is prevent a relationship from beginning in the first place.

Effects of Cortisol on Dopamine Points

Let's say that, for whatever reason, you feel anxiety about the idea of dating someone shorter than you. Let's now say that your tinder date lied about their height and they are actually three inches shorter than you. Height only represents one dopamine category. So, the most you can lose due to cortisol in this area is twice your possible points.

Each of the dopamine categories is only worth a possible 3 points. So, the most negative cortisol points a short person can give you is -6. That means that if your date is breathtaking in every other way, their height won't destroy your interest in them.

What is the problem, however, is that on a first date, all you have is your first impression. How many dopamine categories can you even evaluate in such a short time? Most of them have to do with looks and half of those are probably being obscured by clothing.

That means that if they don't have a balanced face and perfect lips, your short date won't have enough dopamine points to overcome the deduction for their height. That also means that, if they do have a perfectly balanced face and perfect lips, but you don't value those qualities, they won't have enough points to overcome their deduction for height.

Because of these things, a 6 point deduction for height might become a non-starter for you. Is it really a deal-breaker as you might have told friends? Not really. It's just that it's a difficult place to start at considering that a negative dopamine total score will cause you to not want to stay on your date. And if you don't want to be there, you won't continue to discover the characteristics that will give them more dopamine points.

Effects of Cortisol on Oxytocin Points

Since negative cortisol points can be as much as twice the category it's applied to, negative cortisol points can be devastating when applied to your oxytocin points.

Let's say that your partner is beyond emotionally unsupportive. Let's say that they are abusive. They are physically, psychologically, and emotionally abusive. And, let's add that they pressure you to have sex with their friends. That seems horrible right? And any one of good conscience would implore their friend to leave a person like this. The reality, though, is that they don't always leave them. Why is that?

The maximum points you can gain from emotional support is 25 points. That means that the most you can lose from that category are 50 points. That might be a lot, but would it be enough to put the person's overall love score into the negative numbers?

Let's imagine that the person in this nightmare scenario wasn't a friend. And let's say that before meeting their nightmare partner, they were in deep deprivation for all three of the oxytocin categories. That means that, just by spending any time with them, making any contact with them, and by saying anything supportive, the abuser has brought this person back to 0. Bringing them back to 0 will automatically give them 15 points per category and 45 points over all.

And considering that the nightmare partner probably spends a lot of time with them and has sex with them, the nightmare partner is probably significantly in the positive for oxytocin points. Add that to any dopamine points they might also have for looks, and our unfortunate victim is more in love with his abuser than many of us are in love with our spouse.

Like negative dopamine points, negative oxytocin points aren't deal breakers. They are simply obstacles that can be overcome by the addition of positive points from elsewhere.

Calculating your Partner's Negative Cortisol Points

Calculating your partner's negative cortisol points for the dopamine category is pretty straight forward. Simply identify the things about your partner which you would consider to be a turn off. If you are turned off by body hair, for example, then you would separate out all of the area where body hair is found, arms, legs, chest, and back, and then give your partner a negative score between 0 and -6 which reflects how much it makes you not want to be with them.

Keep in mind, this isn't a beauty contest. You aren't rating your partner in comparison to everyone else in the world. What you're doing is identifying the things that make you think about not wanting to be with them. Those same qualities might be what draws other people to them. These aren't necessary qualities that other people dislike about them. These are the things, no matter how superficial, that turns you off about them.

Calculating your partner's negative cortisol points for the oxytocin categories are a little trickier. Again you have to consider the things that your partner does that makes you not want to be with them. This time, however, the areas you should focus on involve the time you spend together, the giving and receiving of emotional support, and contact.

Perhaps the sex isn't fulfilling. How unfulfilling is it? How long has it been unfulfilling?

Perhaps your partner has clammy hands. Perhaps ever time they touch you with those clammy hands you flinch before remembering all of their other fine qualities. From 0 to -50, how much do your partner's clammy hands bother you?

Or, perhaps your partner is unsupportive to the point of making you feel bad about yourself. Give them a score of 0 to -50 for that. Perhaps when you give them emotional support, they barely acknowledge your effort and you feel like you are wasting your time trying to help them. How much does that bother you? Give them a score of 0 to -20 for that.

Negative Cortisol Points	
Negative dopamine points	
Time spent together	
Receiving Emotional support	
Touching	

The above exercise was meant to be fun as well as educational. Honestly, there is no way of determining what your partner's definitive score is. All of our dopamine and oxytocin receptors are different. Some have dopamine receptors which are more sensitive making their dopamine rating of 2 worth more than the same score given by someone who is dopamine insensitive.

But, the reason the above exercise is helpful is that it reveals the areas in which your relationship might be lacking. We are a species which has evolved to fall in love. It might not feel like it right now. But by doing the exercise above, hopefully you've identified untapped love reserves. And I'm also hoping that you're beginning to see how you can find love in spite of the qualities which you might think make you unlovable.

I encourage you to go back and do the exercise again this time evaluating yourself and the things you have to offer others. You only have to get to 100 to inspire love in someone else. Can you get to 100? Remember, the points you get for your looks will naturally decrease over time and your ability to offer emotional support to someone is free. So is your willingness to be there for them when they need you.

Whatever your personal situation is, adding up your, and your partner's love score will help. With the information you gain, you might find areas to exploit in order to get to 100 points. Or, you might discover information that might help you romance your partner.

13
Figuring Out What Romances You and Your Partner

Although I haven't talked about it yet, romance can be an important part of the love game. Some might argue that it is the most important part. I would not. Not because romance isn't important. But because romance is simply a particular combination of everything that has already been discussed.

To show you what I mean, I will first discuss the definition of romance. So, what is romance? What is a romantic gesture? And what is a romantic crush?

What is a Romantic Crush?

Since the concept of romance is a little abstract, it can be more easily explained by first defining an experience that most of us have had. Having a romantic crush was most of our forays into young love. Whether it was for a teen idol or the boy in our class, we've had romantic crushes.

What made our romantic crushes different from other crushes? How does a romantic crush differ from the affection you had for a good friend?

Let's first define romantic crush as a noun.

Definition:
A romantic crush is a person who triggers large amounts of endorphins and oxytocin in you causing you to desire intimate (non-sexual) interactions with them.

<u>What are the defining parts of this definition?</u>
- It is the emphasis on "large" amounts of endorphins and oxytocin.
- It is the focus on interactions that are not related to sex.
- And, it is the desire for intimate interactions.
    - Intimate interactions are interactions which allow the participants to focus on one another while they release oxytocin in each other. (For example, when a restaurant is dimly lit and allows for easy conversation, it is considered a place for intimate interactions.)

Remove any part of that definition and, not only can the type of crush change, but the feelings for the person could stop being romantic and become platonic.

- If a person only triggers the release of small amounts of endorphins an oxytocin, then the dopamine that follows won't make you feel compelled to spend time with them in intimate settings.
- A parent might trigger larger amounts of oxytocin in you and you might desire to have intimate, non-sexual interactions with them, like curling up with them next to a fire. But parents don't usually trigger the release of large amounts of endorphins.
- A best friend might trigger the release of large amounts of oxytocin and endorphins. But until you desire to have intimate interactions with them, they will never exceed the bounds of platonic friendship.

A romantic crush is someone who triggers a strong desire for intimacy but not a strong desire for sex. And, if the intimate interactions you desire involve sex, then there is no need to limit your crush to simply being romantic. It would just be a crush with no qualifier needed.

Now that we've gotten a better understanding of what makes something "romantic", we can go onto the definition of "romancing".

What is Romancing?

Romancing is the initiation of romantic gestures. Romantic gestures *are activities which use intimate interactions to trigger the release of large amounts of endorphins and oxytocin in another*. For example, if you want to romance someone, you might offer this romantic gesture; you might take your partner to a dimly lit Italian restaurant and hold hands across the table as you reveal private details about your life.

This is such an obvious romantic gesture that it nears being a clique. But let's examine this gesture from the perspective of the love game.

In the love game, you are trying to reach 100 points using dopamine and oxytocin points. Dopamine is the neuro-chemical which forces you to focus. A dimly lit restaurant simulates the effects of dopamine by removing visual distractions. That tricks our brain into thinking that it is experiencing a dopamine release. And since the most likely reason for a dopamine release would be because you like them, the experience artificially adds to your love game score.

What also adds to your love game score is the endorphins which are released by eating the tasty food. Remember, we're using dopamine points as a substitute for all of the neuro-chemicals involved with dopamine release. Of those neuro-chemicals, endorphins would be the most important. So when we eat yummy food, it triggers the release of endorphins, which when associated with your date, adds points to your date's dopamine score.

On top of that, being in the same room allows you to look at each other, smell each other and listen to each other. If your date looks, smells and sounds good, it will add to your date's dopamine points.

Holding hands across the table is skin-on-skin contact which gives them more oxytocin points. And them expressing an interest in you adds to your sense of worth and gives them oxytocin points through emotional support.

So, the reason why romancing works is because romantic gestures contribute to your partner's love game score. That means we can draw two conclusions:
- When romantic gestures don't work, it's because they don't generate dopamine and oxytocin points.
- Romantic gestures can be anything that allows the other person to easily focus on you while you trigger a release of oxytocin and endorphins in them.

Why is the second point significant? It's because knowing that will help you to create dates which will better help you win the love game. Not all restaurants simulate the effects of dopamine. Holding hands across the table is not the only way to release oxytocin.

As stated previously, emotional support is a tremendous source of oxytocin points. So, any act of emotional support within an intimate setting which includes the release of dopamine, will count as romancing.

So, let's say that you have ended up with the role of housekeeper in your relationship. Let's say that, not only do you not like doing it, but you feel overwhelmed by all of the work and underappreciated for it.

Now let's say that one night your partner surprises you by feeding you some good food and followed it up with chocolate covered strawberries. Let's add that he puts on your favorite music and precedes to clean the house to show how much he appreciates what you do for him.

That scenario doesn't include a romantic restaurant, or even going out. But if you are feeling overwhelmed and underappreciated for all you do for keeping a nice home, your oxytocin and endorphins will spike like nobody's business.

For that reason, it is important to sit down and figure out what romances you. After all, if you don't know, how is your partner supposed to make you happy? I know that a lot of people employ the 'fumbling in the dark' method when it comes to their own happiness. But that is no way to win the love game.

In the same light, it is important to have a conversation with your partner so that you can figure out what romances them. Here's a hint, areas of oxytocin deficit can often be great romancing targets.

If your partner feels that their parents didn't give them enough time as a child, there is a strong likelihood that the most effective romantic gesture will involve you spending a lot of time on them. Perhaps they might appreciate you making them a desert that takes hours to prepare. Or, perhaps organizing an outing which is filled with details that clearly takes a long time to plan, is a better way to go.

If your partner feels that they weren't made to feel like they mattered to their parents, then gestures which involve showing them how much you matter to them would be effective. Giving them flowers might show that. Spending large sums of money on them might show that. Or, simply getting them into an intimate setting and listing examples of how much they matter to you, could send their oxytocin and endorphin levels skyrocketing.

The point is that you will never know these things until you sit down and figure these things out. And once you have figured out what romances you and your partner, you can use that information to get to, or remain at 100 points.

14
Revitalizing A Stale Relationship

There is no shame in becoming bored with your partner. At the same time, it is not an inevitable outcome. It is also doesn't have to be a permanent state.

We become bored with our partner for one reason, the decrease in oxytocin and dopamine points. If it is early in your relationship, within 6 months, the culprit is usually a drop in dopamine points. If you have survived the natural decline in dopamine points and have had a love score consisting of mostly oxytocin points, then your relationship's decline is most likely due to a decline in oxytocin points.

Although it's possible to recover from either situation, there is one situation which is easier to fix than the other.

Revitalizing Your Oxytocin Points

A relationship based on oxytocin points can be a satisfying one. The only downside is that, unless you are wired to be emotionally supportive, it can require a lot of work to maintain.

At the beginning of a relationship, it's easy to care about your partner's day. You will get rewarded with dopamine points just by the smile your partner gets when you ask them. After 6 months or a year, those free dopamine points are gone. Now, you just need to ask your partner about their day because you know it matters to them.

Will your gesture of emotional support benefit you in the end? Yes. The more love points your partner has for you, the more likely they are to support you when you need it and to give you those wonderful skin-on-skin contact points. They might even decide to have sex with you.

But, as the dopamine points diminish from sex, you might really wonder if all of the effort is worth it. And, aren't you tired from your own hard day at work? Wouldn't a night of getting lost in video games do more to revitalize you than sex or emotional support?

After all, video games have one purpose, to spike dopamine. Your partner doesn't have that as their sole purpose. And really, doesn't a revitalized partner benefit everyone in the relationship? Isn't your getting lost in a video game what's best for everyone in the long run?

Yes, it is very easy to rationalize why you've stopped offering emotional support to your partner, or why you've stopped making contact with them. We all have busy lives and needs that need fulfilling. But when you stop doing the things that gave you all of your original oxytocin points, your oxytocin score will drop.

Will it drop so low that you will feel like you're living with a platonic roommate? Maybe. Will it drop so low that your relationship will no longer feel like it's worth the effort? Possibly. Was your relationship a key source of life score points? And now that your oxytocin points have dropped, do you now feel unhappy about life in general? That could definitely happen.

So, what are you to do? The answer is, sit down, add up your partner's oxytocin and dopamine scores and figure out where you can get more points. This is a tricky task to do on your own. And, you might think that the only thing you have sole control over is how much time you two spend together. Is that true though?

Remember that, although you might get more points when someone touches you, you do also get points when you touch someone else. You also get points when you make extended eye contact with your partner.

Granted, if your partner is in a deficit state for contact and you suddenly start touching them, they might think that you are initiating more than you are. Also, if your partner no longer feels a dopamine rush from your touch, they might recoil from your touch in fear of what you might be trying to initiate.

The only way through either scenario is to push through. Make touching your partner a regular activity once again. Teach them that a touch is sometimes just a touch. If you do that, they will eventually receive a release of oxytocin from it just like you do. And like that, you have begun to revitalize your relationship.

Being emotionally supportive to your partner can also be a source of oxytocin points. This is a little trickier because you only get those points if you see that your efforts have made a difference. But if your partner once rewarded you for your emotional support, they are capable of doing it again.

It might take them a while to remember that. And, them remembering may require a gentle reminder from you. But human nature says that we naturally do good things for others when they do good things for us.

If, on the other hand, there has been a buildup of negative cortisol points between you and your partner, things can get trickier still. Negative cortisol points are distributed for a reason. People tend to earn the negative cortisol points you give them, just like you earn the ones you get.

If you're in a relationship with a partner who doesn't readily share their feelings, getting them to talk about the negative cortisol points they have given you might be difficult. They might not even know they've done it. But as long as those negative cortisol points exist, your overall oxytocin points are only going down. And it is in situations like this that visiting a therapist might be your only option.

A therapist might be able to address your specific situations and challenges while creating a safe environment for you both to express yourselves. Even with a therapist, you can't expect, miracles, however.

Remember, humans with large amounts of testosterone process emotions differently than humans with large amounts of estrogen. Those two groups simply experience life and emotions in different ways. Can you two return to a state where things were wonderful? Of course. It just requires a willingness to put in the necessary work to get there.

Revitalizing Your Dopamine Points

As a person who is considered dopamine insensitive, this topic is near and dear to my heart. A dopamine insensitive person can so easily be seduced by all of the readily available dopamine points that they will often stack their love game score with it.

The newness of it all is amazing! The novelty of the sex is amazing! Add in the points from their balanced face and physical forms and you can get to 100 points in no time.

This relationship has no future, however. Humans have evolved in a way to guarantee that dopamine points will decline over time. You could be in a relationship with the most beautiful person in the world. But, as long as you keep spending time with them, eventually, you will get bored of them.

So, is there anything that can be done for a relationship that was based on dopamine points alone?

Perhaps there's one thing. Your partner could become the source of new dopamine points. Dopamine points aren't only distributed for what someone looks like, they can be distributed to your partner because of the experiences they give you.

If you receive dopamine from travel and your partner enables you to travel by paying for it, or organizing it, or just by coming with you, you will give them dopamine points for it. If you get large spikes of endorphins from wonderful food and your partner either cooks it for you, finds the dining experiences, or pays for it for you, you will give them the dopamine points associated with the experience. And if you get huge amounts of dopamine from having sex with a new partner and your partner facilitates that for you, you will, believe it or not, associate the resulting dopamine points to your partner for facilitating it.

Those are examples of how you could revitalize your dopamine points in a relationship based solely on dopamine points. However, the most effective way to revitalize a relationship which is mostly based on dopamine points would be to mine all of the untapped oxytocin points available to you.

For some, none of the options offered above will be helpful. In many cases, your best option will be to let this particular game session end and then start over with a new player. Why might it be preferable to concede defeat and to begin again? Let's discuss that.

15
Know When To Concede Defeat

As any experienced gamer will tell you, no matter how good you are, you are not going to win every game. Sure, your goal might be to win every time, but it is impossible. Sometimes you start playing without even knowing the rules. How can you realistically expect to win if you don't know the moves you can and cannot make?

Another thing which will guarantee defeat is playing with a bad partner. Listen, I personally have, and have always had many wonderful attributes. I've always been caring and loyal. I've always been interesting to talk to and fairly easy on the eyes. But, up until a few years ago, any woman who hoped to win the love game playing with me as a partner was guaranteed to lose.

I, simply, could not trust others enough to allow them to give me emotional support. I also had a huge secret. Hiding my bisexuality took a lot out of me and it caused me to want to limit how intimate I was with my partner, and how much time I spent with them.

The result was that every love game I engaged in was overloaded with dopamine points. And once those dopamine points naturally declined, my relationships came to an abrupt end.

Was there anything my partners could have done to facilitate my trust? Sure, but they would have had to have been a miracle worker. They would have had to thread that needle like a master tailor.

And, even then, could they guaranteed a successful outcome. Hell no. I simply wasn't capable of being in an oxytocin based relationship before recently. And anyone who might have tried to have one with me would have failed.

I share this unfortunate fact about my past because I know I'm not the only one for which this is true. This could be true for you. This could be true for your last boyfriend or girlfriend. And it doesn't matter whether the person was willing to marry you or not. There are people in this world, who because of their current circumstances, are incapable of winning the love game.

Will they always be a bad love game partner? Maybe. Maybe not. There is no way to tell.

Can you be the one to change them into to perfect partner? Maybe. Maybe not.

If your relationship isn't currently working, should you breakup? Maybe. I don't know your current situation, so how could I know that?

What I can say is that when a relationship isn't working, it is often the fault of both partners. That's not always true, however. Sometimes it's your partner's fault. Sometimes it's yours. Certainly, none of my previous partners were perfect players, but my presence made winning the game impossible.

It might be worth it to ask yourself if you are capable of reaching 100 points with any partner. If so, what type of partner would it take? Does that type of person exist in real life?

If they do, where would you find them? And if any of those answers lead you away from your current partner, maybe it's time to concede defeat for this round before finding a new partner and starting again.

16
Dealing With Heartbreak

Love is a tricky game. But, when you're winning, it feels amazing. What that also means, however, is that when you're losing it, it's the worst feeling in the world.

Why does heartbreak hurt so much? It's the withdrawal pangs. Defining love as the accumulation of 100 points puts the love experience in a certain category. At those levels, love is pretty similar to the most addictive drugs. And, of course, it is.

There isn't a separate part of your brain designated to being addicted to crack cocaine and heroin versus love. It's all the same parts. It's even all of the same mechanisms.

Crack cocaine is addictive because it spikes your dopamine receptors to such a degree that the receptors down regulate. If you remember my sound mixer and singer analogy, that means that once the levels have been lowered, our singer will have to scream into her microphone to be heard at a normal volume by the audience.

How does that relate to down regulated dopamine receptors when using crack? It means that in order to feel anywhere near normal after using crack a couple of times, you need to do something to spike your dopamine in a similar way.

And what happens if you can't get an intense spike of dopamine? Your dopamine receptors enter a deficit state in which you can't receive enough pleasure from any of the normal things in life.

Those same mechanisms are in play with the love game. If your dopamine points decline slowly over time, your dopamine receptors have time to readjust as your dopamine points drop. But if the source of your dopamine points is ripped from you while you are in an addicted state, you will suddenly be thrown into a deficit.

Without the ability to experience pleasure, you will feel numb. The only thing you can do is the same as any crack addict, wait it out and hope you don't relapse. You will find it near impossible to not think about your beloved crack, but you will have to get your mind off of it to recover.

You also have to keep in mind that you don't actually need that person to feel pleasure again. What you're hungry for is dopamine. That can be gained from multiple sources. The healthier ones are sporting competitions, video games, and work achievements. The unhealthier ones are alcohol, sugar, and gambling. Choose wisely or none at all.

The reason why heartbreak physically hurts, however, is not because of the dopamine withdrawal pangs. That ache in your chest and inability to breath is due to your opioid addiction. Just like there are endorphin receptors in your brain, there are opioid receptors. And just like endorphins are counted under your dopamine points, opioids are counted under your oxytocin points.

And if you recognize the word 'opioid', it's because you should. Opioids are a certain class of drug which includes heroin and oxycodone. They are the stars of America's current opioid crisis. And the neuro-chemicals involved with oxytocin points work on the same brain receptors, in a similar way.

When you are in love, it can feel like you do when you're in the throes of heroin. And when your heroin supply is taken from you, it can feel the way you do from a breakup.

The physical pain you feel, however, comes from an opioids ability to relieve pain. A part of the heroin high involves the deadening of the body's nerve receptors. So, when you are suddenly thrown into an opioid deficit, your pain receptors are made more sensitive. The result is pain that is identical to any physical injury.

The pain can hurt so bad that it becomes hard to breath. It can sap you of your strength and your will to live. Add that to a thirst for dopamine which cannot be quenched and you are in a really bad state.

But, just like on the dopamine side of things, it's important to remember that it isn't the person that you need. It's that glorious hit of opioids and oxytocin. Your brain receptors can't tell the difference in the source of the drug. It just needs its receptor's filled.

Again, the best thing you can do in this situation is to wait out the addiction. Yes, it hurts, but this too shall pass. When it does, you will barely remember how bad it was.

As opposed to just waiting it out, you can also replace your source of opioids with another. There is an oxytocin nasal spray that you can buy over the counter. It isn't even close to the rush you'll get from being in love, but it could facilitate the formation of new bonds. Whether it's a new partner or helping you reconnect with your friends, a few shots of an oxytocin nasal spray may help you transition through the stages of your oxytocin withdrawal.

17
How To Give Emotional Support

As a final tip, I thought I would discuss something which might seem obvious but isn't. That is, how to give emotional support. But, before I do, I'll remind you what emotional support is.

I have defined emotional support as engaging in actions that contribute to a person's sense of worth. That is easy to say, but what does that really mean? And, what are examples?

Anywhere that discusses how to give emotional support will generally focus on doing two things, listening to the person, and offering physical contact like a hug. Those are wonderful forms of emotional support and they fit within the definition.

Both listening and hugging are actions. The act of listening to someone as they share their dilemmas says to the speaker that you think they are valuable enough to devote your time to. That's a powerful message, especially if their dilemma involves them being made to feel like they don't have value.

The other action is giving a hug. It could also be a light touch on the forearm or a hand on the person's shoulder. The touch itself will release oxytocin which, on its own, will help the other person feel better. But the empathy that often accompanies such a touch, again communicates the message that their emotions have an impact on you, and hence matters. Empathy is a powerful signal of worth.

Listening and hugging are not the only things you can do as emotional support, however. And, in many cases, they aren't even the most effective thing.

With emotional support, the goal is to contribute to your partner's sense of worth. Worth isn't just one thing in one area, though. Worth is a concept that can be targeted on multiple topics. You can have a high sense of worth about your contribution at work while feeling a deficit of worth when it comes to whether or not you should be loved.

Or, you could feel a high sense of worth about your place within platonic friendships, but not have a sense of worth when it comes to romantic relationships. Listening to someone as they talk about their challenges seems to offer some affirmation of worth no matter what the topic. But there are actions that can be tailored to the situation your partner is experiencing.

As an example, let's say that your partner feels diminished at work because no one ever returns their texts or emails. And, let's say that they text that message to you. What action would most contribute to their sense of worth?

Well, if the source of their emotional distress comes from no one valuing them enough to text them back, then wouldn't texting them your reply as quickly as possible contribute the most to their sense of worth? That could be a form of listening to them, but the primary contribution from your action is your underlying message. By texting them quickly, you are showing them that, even if they don't have worth in their co-workers' eyes, they have worth in your eyes.

As another example, let's say that your girlfriend is currently having a really hard time with life. Let's say that her business is failing, she is having an existential crisis about her place in the world, and she is feeling lost. Yes, listening to her as she shares her problems would give her a sense that, in spite of everything, she still has someone who cares. But, is there something you can do that would more effectively contribute to her sense of worth?

It seems to me that your girlfriend's mayor dilemma is that she is feeling lost. We've all been there. It feels like you're losing your firm grip on your life. You don't know what you should trust anymore or if anything matters.

What would contribute the most to your girlfriend's sense of worth in this case? Helping her to reestablish her grounding. Perhaps you can arrange for a get together of the people who have always given her a sense of belonging. It could be her parents or her long time best friends. If she felt the most ground at college, perhaps you can arrange a quick trip back.

Certainly, this is a little more work than just listening to her as she shares her daily dilemmas, but how much more effective would something like this be in contributing to her sense of worth?

My final example will involve something which is very common in relationships. Let's say that your boyfriend has constant trust issues because they had an ex cheat on them. This is something that many of us have faced.

Yes, you can listen to them when they talk to you about how they felt when you did something that triggered them, and that will give them some sense of relief. But wouldn't it contribute more to their sense of worth to take an action that gets to the heart of their dilemma?

More than most things, cheating can attack a person's sense of worth. What is it that does that? Is it the sex? Not implicitly. There are millions of people in open or polyamorous relationships and their partner's extra-marital affairs do nothing to shake the bond in the primary relationship.

What is most damaging when it comes to cheating is what people believe the cheating says about them. People interrupt the cheating as a confirmation of their lack of worth. They aren't worth enough to remain loyal to. They aren't doing a good enough job in the bedroom. Or, they take it as a sign of their lack of worth in the world.

What could you do or say that might contribute the most to their sense of worth in this case? You could remind them of their qualities which will remain independent of whether or not someone cheats on them.

Do you believe they're beautiful? Do you believe they're smart? Remind them of the things that give them worth. Tell them that they will have that in spite of their partner's fidelity. And build them up as an entity which has worth outside of the actions of others.

You're not going to fix them overnight by saying this. But, will it do a lot to heal the wound they're nursing?

Definitely. And will it more effectively contribute to their sense of worth than simply listening to them or offering them a hug when their insecurities flare up? Absolutely.

If you want a fall back strategy on how to give your partner emotional support, you can always just listen to them when they need someone to talk to and be quick to offer them a hug. But if you are looking for a way to build up your own love score within your partner's mind, you can think a little outside the box and take into account the issue which is causing them distress.

Do this and you will be the best boyfriend, girlfriend, husband, or wife ever. And by doing this, you'll be a lot closer to having 100 points, and getting your partner to fall head over heels in love with you.

18
Wrapping up

In spite of the myth surrounding it, the love game isn't difficult to understand. Human beings are animals driven by a reward system whose primary purpose is to bond and procreate. Although your particular circumstance my vary from the examples I've mentioned above, it isn't going to vary by that much.

We all react to physical and psycho-social traits within each other. The traits we like will result in dopamine spikes. Unless we have a mental condition that prevents it, we will respond positively to spending time with, giving and receiving emotion support from, and from eye and skin-on-skin contact with those we like.

We will feel driven to maximize pleasure, and because of our evolution, we will feel less pleasure from the same stimuli over time. That is true for all of the things that spike our dopamine. And that is true for things like touching which initially spikes both dopamine and oxytocin but will only spike oxytocin over time.

We are both a simple and complex beast. But given the understanding that the 100 point love game gives you, you can begin to construct the scenario that will bring you the most happiness. You don't have to do all of the things I've mentioned above. But within it, you can empower yourself to create the life you want.

I hope that my understanding of the love game gives you as much relief as it has given me. And as you use it to create your ideal life, remember that there is no right or wrong way to be. There are only actions that bring you closer to 100 points and behaviors that help you win the love game.

www.ingramcontent.com/pod-product-compliance
Lightning Source LLC
LaVergne TN
LVHW041608070526
838199LV00052B/3032